AF228365

RIDICULOUS RIDDLES

JOKE BOOK

Lisa Regan

WINDMILL BOOKS

Published in 2020 by Windmill Books,
an Imprint of Rosen Publishing
29 East 21st Street, New York, NY 10010

Cataloging-in-Publication Data

Names: Regan, Lisa.
Title: Ridiculous riddles joke book / Lisa Regan.
Description: New York : Windmill Books, 2020. | Series: Sidesplitting jokes | Includes glossary and index.
Identifiers: ISBN 9781725396029 (pbk.) | ISBN 9781725396043 (library bound) | ISBN 9781725396036 (6 pack)
Subjects: LCSH: Riddles, Juvenile. | Wit and humor, Juvenile.
Classification: LCC PN6371.5 R465 2020 | DDC 398'.6--dc23

Manufactured in the United States of America

CPSIA Compliance Information: Batch BW20WM: For Further Information contact
Rosen Publishing, New York, New York at 1-800-237-9932

WARNING!

this book is dangerously funny!

Are you ready for the best selection of funny stuff ever gathered together under one cover? Prepare yourself for a heap of brand new jokes, a pile of classic sidesplitters, and a big bundle of laughs. It all adds up to a stack of fun to share with your friends and family. Warn them to find a safe place to listen, as they'll soon be laughing their heads off!

How can you tell which of your friends has upgraded their phone?
Don't worry, they'll tell you!
What do ghosts use to call their friends?
A terror-phone.
What about skeletons?
They use a tele-bone!
How does a parent find out where their kid is?
They turn off the wi-fi and see where the noise comes from!
Why was the computer late for work?
It had a hard drive.

Did you hear about the phones that fell in love?

They exchanged rings!

How can you tell when a bee is on the line?

You get a buzzy signal!

Why did the phone wear glasses?
It had lost its contacts!

How do you keep your phone from breaking if you drop it?

Keep it in flight mode!

What do you call a man who jokes all the time? Josh.
What do you call a man who is tall enough to see over a crowd? Isaiah.
What do you call a man who carries a shovel? Doug.
What do you call someone who sees an Apple store get robbed? An iWitness.

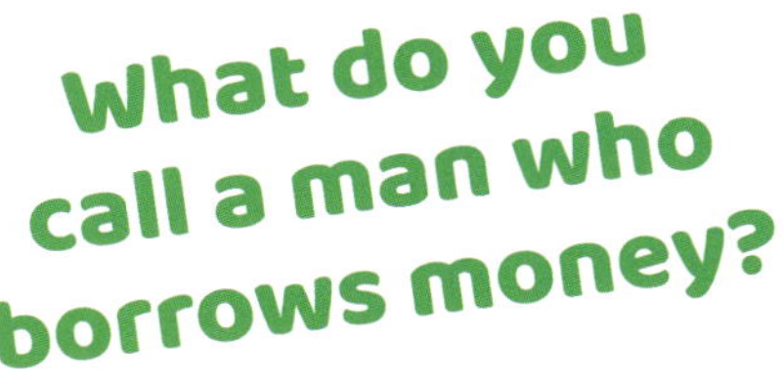

What do you call a man who borrows money?

Owen.

What do you call a man who tries to trick you?

Connor.

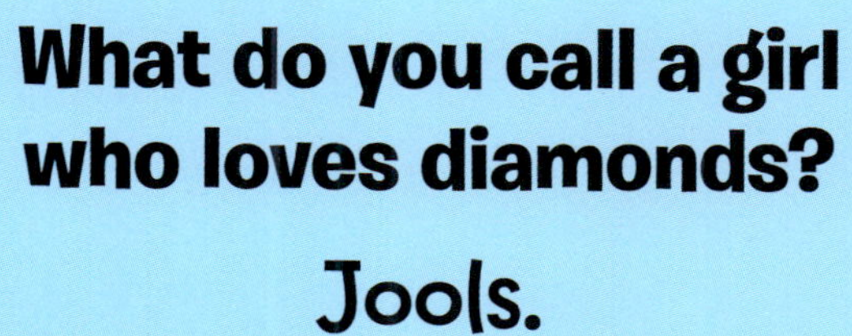
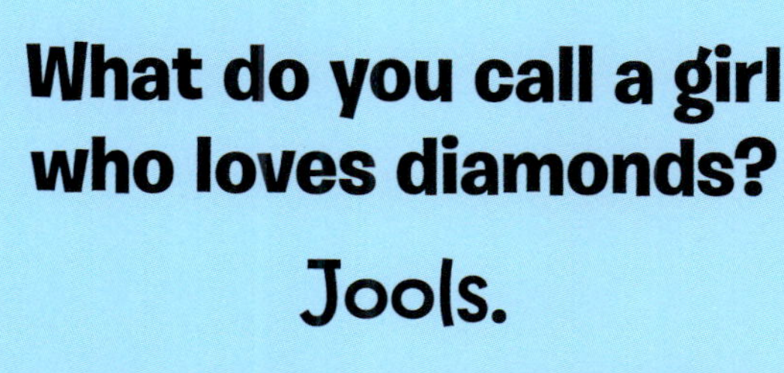

What do you call a girl who loves diamonds?

Jools.

What do you call a man who never tells the truth?

Eli.

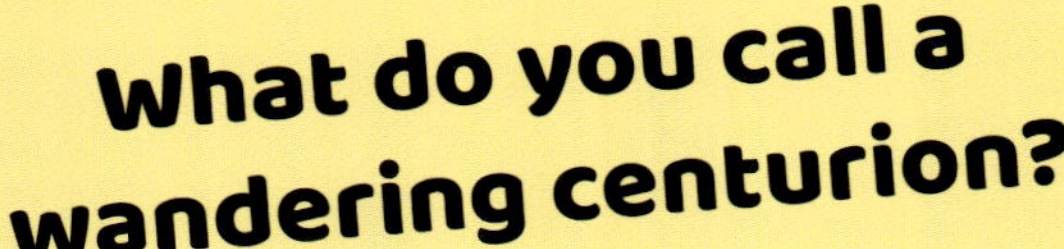

What do you call a wandering centurion?

A roamin' soldier.

Why didn't they film *Lord of the Rings* in Antarctica?

It's uninhobbitable.

What did the scientist say when she combined oxygen and magnesium?

OMg!

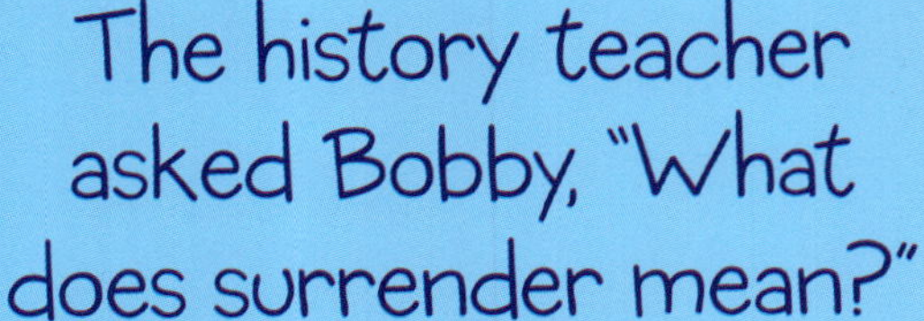

The history teacher asked Bobby, "What does surrender mean?"

Bobby replied, "I give up!"

Why can't you trust atoms?

They make up everything!

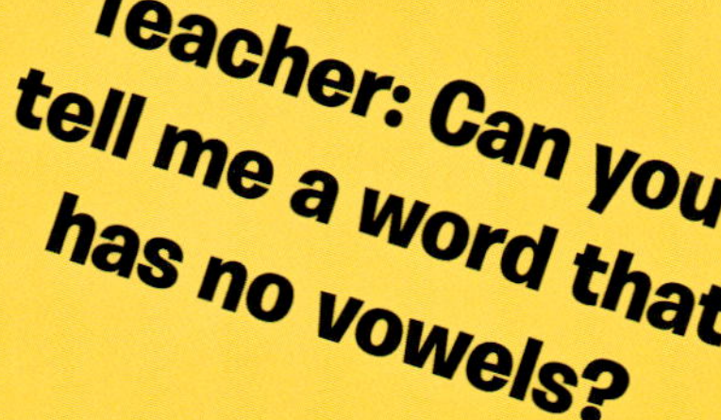

Teacher: Can you tell me a word that has no vowels?

Abby: Why?

What do you call a shade of blue that doesn't exist except in your dreams?

A pigment of your imagination.

How far can you throw an envelope?

As far as you like, but it will still be stationery.

Why did the star
go to school?

To get brighter!

Where would an astronaut leave
his spaceship?
At a parking meteor!

Where do astronauts put
their dinners?

In satellite dishes.

When do astronauts
eat their sandwiches?

At launch time!

How do you get a baby
astronaut to sleep?

Rocket.

How do you
know when
the moon had
enough to eat?

When it's full!

How many
astronauts can
you fit in a
rocket ship?

As many as you
like – you'll never
run out of space!

Why is it cheap to feed a giraffe?
A little goes a long way!

What did the girl say when she returned from a once-in-a-lifetime trip?
Never again.

Why didn't the viper vipe 'er nose?
Because the adder 'ad 'er 'ankerchief!

Will your dad get angry if you take that kitchen utensil?
I dunno, but it's a whisk I'm willing to take.

What do you say when a man throws cheese and milk at you?

How dairy?

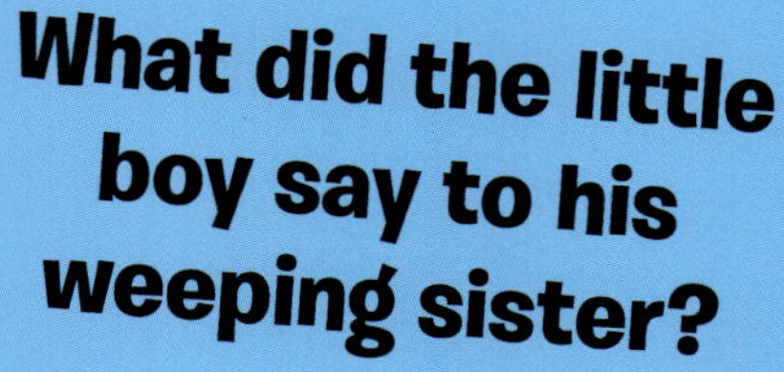

What did the little boy say to his weeping sister?

Don't have a cry, sis!

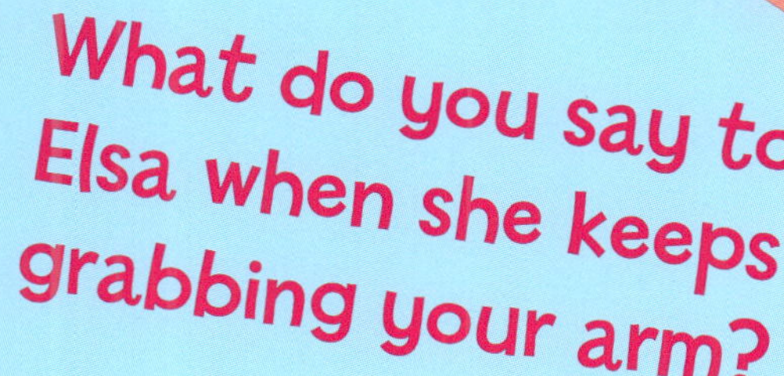

What do you say to Elsa when she keeps grabbing your arm?

Let it go!

What did the traffic light say to the car?

Don't look now, I'm changing!

What sport does an elephant love to play?
Squash!
What do you get if you cross a river and a lake?
Wet!
What do you get if you cross a bird, a vehicle, and a dog?
A flying car-pet.
What do you get if you cross a frog with a rabbit?
A bunny ribbit!

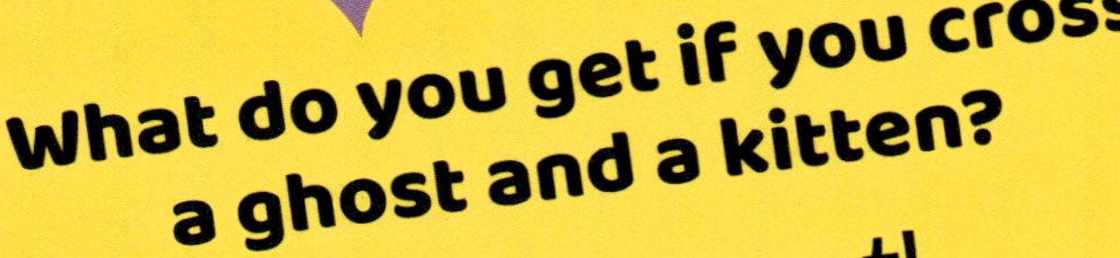

What do you get if you cross a rooster and a bell?

An alarm cluck!

What do you get if you cross a parrot and a lion?

A creature that will talk your ear off!

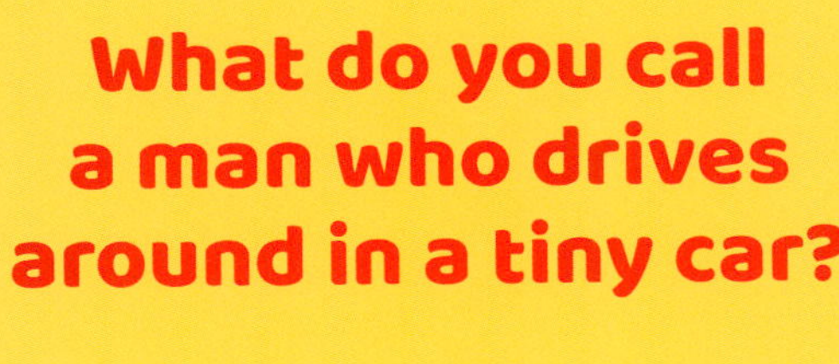

What do you call
a man who drives
around in a tiny car?

Carter.

What do you call a man
with a toilet on his head?

John!

What do you call a relative
with six legs?

Ant.

What do you call
a woman with
one short leg?

Eileen.

What do you call a man who can decorate your bathroom?

Tyler.

What do you call a man with a map on his head?

Miles!

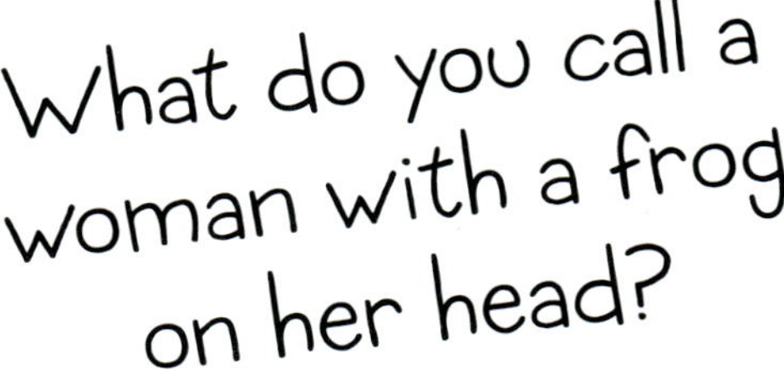

What do you call a woman with a frog on her head?

Lily!

What do you call a man who can sing really loudly?

Mike.

What did the gardener say to her boyfriend?
You're really growing on me!
What flowers grow under your nose?
Tulips.
What did one toilet say to the other?
You look flushed!
Why can't a hand be twelve inches long?
Because then it would be a foot!

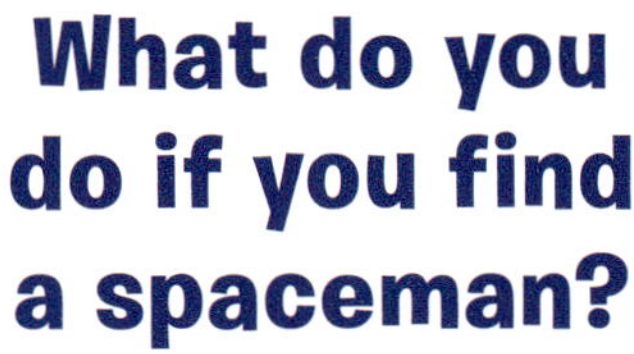

What do you do if you find a spaceman?

You park in it, man!

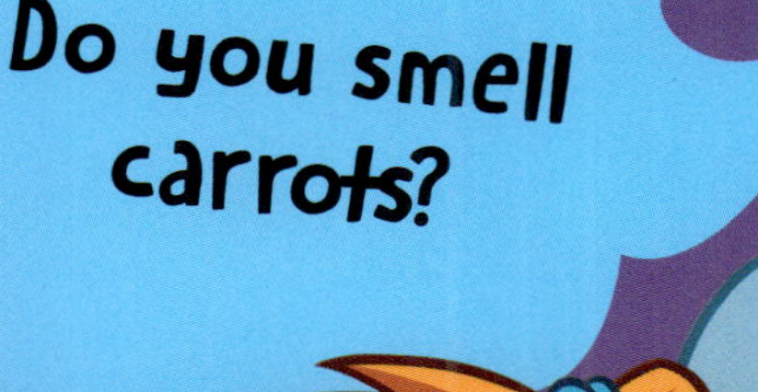

What did the snowman say to his friend?

Do you smell carrots?

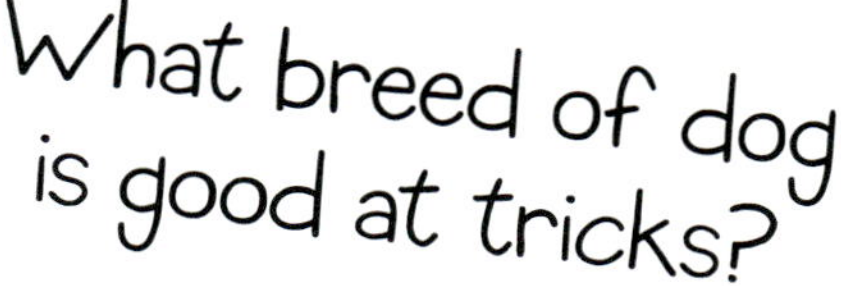

What breed of dog is good at tricks?

A Labra-cadabra-dor.

Why couldn't the bicycle stand up on its own?

It was too tire-d.

Why are rock stars always cool?
Because they have so many fans!
Why did the scarecrow win an award?
He was outstanding in his field!
Why did the burglar take a bath?
He wanted to make a clean getaway!
Why should you never tell secrets in a vegetable garden?
Because potatoes have eyes, and beanstalk.

What do lawyers wear for work?
Lawsuits.
What did the roofer say to his first customer?
This one's on the house!
What did the limo driver say when he retired without a pension?
All those years, and nothing to chauffeur it.
What kind of award does a dentist receive?
A little plaque.

What do you call a camel with no humps?
Humphrey.
What do you call a man who runs faster than you?
Chase.
What's as big as a T. rex, but doesn't weigh anything at all?
A T. rex's shadow.
Why won't you believe that I can touch my toes?
It's too much of a stretch.

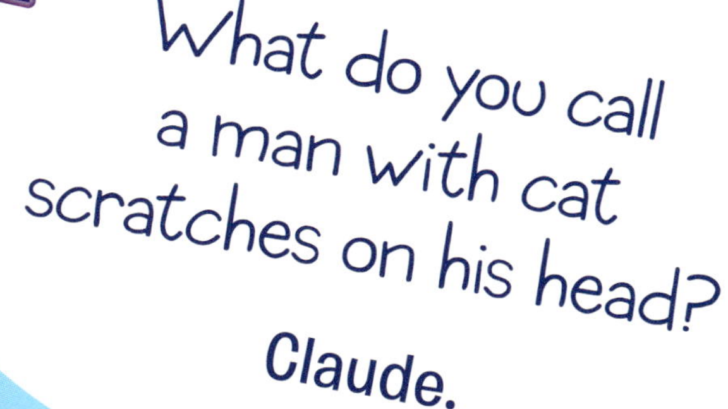
What do you call a man who can lift up a car?
Jack.
What do you call a man with cat scratches on his head?
Claude.

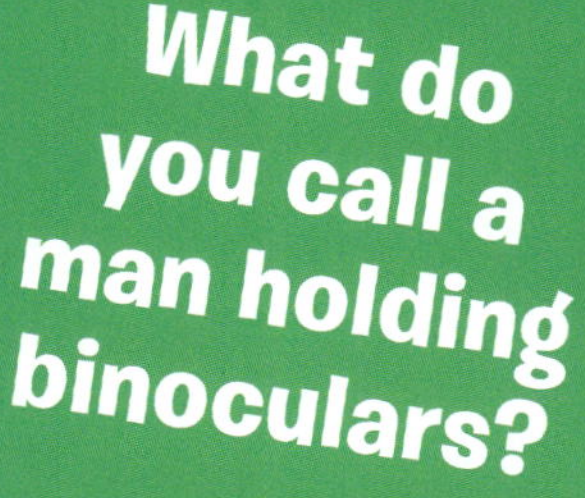
What do you call a man holding binoculars?
Luke Farther.

What do you call a man who sits in front of the door?
Matt.

Glossary

atom The smallest amount of a substance that can take part in a chemical reaction.

centurion A Roman soldier.

flight mode A setting for cell phones when used on an airplane.

lawsuit A court case concerning a dispute between two people or organizations.

meteor A piece of rock or metal that burns brightly when it enters Earth's atmosphere from space.

pigment A substance that gives something a particular color.

Index